THE MINISTRY
TO
THE DIVORCED

Joseph E. Norris

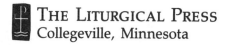
THE LITURGICAL PRESS
Collegeville, Minnesota

CONTENTS

Cover design by Ann Blattner. Photo by Cleo Freelance Photography.

1   2   3   4   5   6   7   8   9   10

Preface

This manual is about what I have managed to learn from the people who ministered to me on my own way through the process of recovery and healing from divorce. I would like to acknowledge a few of them here. Sr. Jane McKinlay, R.S.C.J., the director of divorce ministry for the archdiocese of San Francisco, has blessed more people's lives than anyone I know, has somehow managed the miracle of being the heart and soul of our ministry without detracting from its being our own ministry, and has made herself a dear friend. Pat Galli, former Region XI Representative for the North American Conference of Separated and Divorced Catholics, is the example I have most in mind when I talk about leadership by empowerment; Phil Correa, her successor, has served admirably for my example in empowerment by activation. Fr. Al Grosskopf, S.J., who was a pioneer in divorce ministry for the San Francisco Bay Area and still inspires us all to keep on plugging, is also a master practitioner of the healing presence. Sr. Lorita Moffatt, S.M., the chaplain and moderator of the New Dimensions Support Group at St. Stephen's parish in San Francisco, has provided invaluable precept and example in every aspect of what ministry is about. Janet Arpin and Joe Brunato, fellow members and my predecessors in leading my support group, have earned my profound gratitude in their ways of modelling the process, being there when it mattered, and spending endless hours in the nearly lost art of good conversation. And the couple of hundred people who have cycled through our group on their ways to wholeness have woven a particularly rich and lovely bit in the tapestry of creation; they will forever be my cherished notion of what the Church is all about.

Joseph E. Norris

Introduction

There was a time when stability in marriage was a hallmark of the Catholic Church, one of the things we would point out to show that we were something special. No more; for some time now our marital failure rate has been the same as that of the secular population around us. This is a scandal and a sign of something gone terribly wrong within the Church. It means that in what we have always considered a key area we have now lost our effect on our own people, let alone on the community at large. It means the vocation through which most of us used to be called to sanctity has been effectively closed to half of those who attempt it. It means, in short, that the Church in America is in serious trouble! The United States Bishops' Conference recognized this through the urgent tone of documents as early as the 1978 pastoral letter on family life ministry, and in the activities of the diocesan tribunals—their case load, and the number of decrees of nullity issued, are not just rubber stamps of civil divorce but recognition of the underlying crisis. Divorce ministry is not just another organization; it addresses a problem that threatens our integrity as an institution, and besides plugging a very large leak in the Bark of Peter, so to speak, it points the way to removing the cause and conducting ourselves so as not to repeat it.

Let me illustrate that point with the perhaps apocryphal story of the management consultant who had occasion to remind his client, a manufacturer of drill bits, that the customer couldn't care less about the drill bit; all he wanted was the hole. It seems to some of us that it is time to ask ourselves what the Church is here to provide: "drill bits" (the visible, bureaucratic organization with its programs and projects) or "holes" (healing for broken souls in need of salvation). If the latter, then the ministry by and among divorced Catholics, as described in this manual, comes into its own. The small-group format on which it is based can respond to the individual soul's needs in real time when it counts and is inherently less likely than our traditionally large organizations to confuse the issue by looking to its own formal perfection instead of the customer's needs. It tends also to hold most effectively to the principle so vividly set out in 1 Corinthians 12—that we are the Body of Christ, member by member—and so to mobilize each of us in using our God-given talents rightly for the benefit of the whole Christian community as well as for our own healing. We might want to keep this in mind when we contrast our own institutional woes with the way some of our evangelical Protestant brethren seem to thrive, high standards and all, in the same hostile secular community.

Those are strong words that will doubtless give offense, but they are necessary in view of the undeniable and highly visible crisis in our family life. However, let me stress that I do not in any way wish to criticize the Church institution as such. Church history has always been about the dynamic tension between the need for imaginative zeal and the equal need for structure and stability. The wildeyes and the bureaucrats need each other to keep themselves on track, and the issue between them is of personalities and working styles, not of faith and morals. That is the case here; my point, as a wildeye, is that we need to look at our balance, but that nothing in the family crisis, grave as it is, calls for more than a historically routine checking of perspectives.

Let me digress to emphasize that when we talk about "Divorce Ministry" we are talking about healing the effects of civil divorce and addressing its causes. We do not advocate civil divorce as a cure for life's troubles; the Christian Sacrament of Matrimony is always and for everyone a call to a heroic life with all that means in routine difficulties and sacrifice. It often happens that persons newly separated or contemplating a break attend a few of our meetings, get an earful of what awaits them on the road through divorce, and opt for reconciliation. There are times, however, when there is no choice, as when one's spouse departs either physically or morally (a husband who beats his wife has departed morally, for instance), or when it becomes obvious that the marriage simply does not exist because one or both spouses failed to make the commitment (see below, in the section on the tribunal).

Whatever the circumstances, please get it straight that while the Lord can turn anything to good, divorce itself is always a disaster and that our ministry is concerned with our brothers' and sisters' pain after it has befallen them, without judgement about how it happened. We have set out to be healers, not confessors.

Let us also keep it clear throughout this discussion that divorced people are ordinary sinners like the rest of us, only sometimes a bit more obviously so. Divorce ministry can be of enormous benefit to the Church at large, but it will be so by clarifying for all of us what the Church at large is here to do, not by containing anyone wiser or holier than the rest.

Finally, please observe the vital distinction between civil divorce, which is about the financial and child custody settlements of people no longer living together, and a Church annulment, which is about their status in the eyes of God. A civil divorce per se is a non-event in the eyes of the Church; it is civil divorce *and remarriage without recourse to the tribunal* that is forbidden to Catholics, not the divorce alone. We will discuss this more fully later, but meanwhile it will help to avoid confusion if we keep our terms straight.

The idea of a divorce ministry for Catholics is still relatively new. We constantly meet people who are amazed to hear that any such thing exists. That means the field is still in its initial phase of rapid growth, with many issues still open. This manual reflects one of many local options, based on what we find works for us, but be aware that other approaches exist. The final word on this field is still far in the future; you can take pride in your place at the leading edge of a very important bit of Church history. May your rewards be commensurate with the challenges you will face as you fill in your part of the picture!

1

The Church and Marriage

Importance of Marriage to the Mission of the Church

In chapter 5 of his Letter to the Ephesians, Paul makes his famous equation of family to Church and vice versa. Marriage, as a vocation to a specific way to be saved, is at the center of the storm, swept by all the cross-currents that have so disturbed us recently. As the Church goes, so marriage goes. That is why divorce is not just another item in the long list of crises: it comprehends all of those things and more besides. In the same way the pressure on today's lay Catholic to fill the vacuums left by the scarcity of priests and religious and the fading of traditional Church culture, just when their absence is most sorely felt, has been brought to bear most of all on the Christian family. This is at once a serious threat and a glorious opportunity.

If marriage is indeed the Church in microcosm, if it is the way along which most of us are invited to walk with the Lord, then success in marriage and in Church life alike will depend on our vision of what the Gospel is all about. Lacking that vision, we have cohabitation but not Christian marriage, congregation but no community; no ifs, ands, or buts. Apart from that vision, the words of the popes on the family and its importance and the right way to order it will seem naive, impractical, and downright fatuous. With that vision, those same words will show themselves loaded with sharp-edged pragmatism. The difference is simply in whether my walk with the Lord is or is not the most important thing in the world for me. If it is, I will see the world and all that is in it one way; if not, I inhabit a totally different universe, and the gulf between the two really is absolute. When we say Christian marriage is a vocation, we mean it is specifically designed by Divine Providence to confront me with that gulf and to keep me in that confrontation until the old Adam is gone and the new Christ is completely put on—or until I have definitively rejected his way.

Contemporary Trends Against Christian Marriage

The Objectified Other

Such talk will not go down at all well with our "Me Generation" and its fixation with the latest yuppie toy. The mentality that sees a spouse as a sort of life-size barbie doll will not easily grasp the Christian vision. Nor will the attitude that talks of relating as "an experience," as if a love affair were some sort of touchie-feelie movie. That distancing and objectifying, so typical of today's First World mindset, run directly counter to the growth in intimacy of two souls learning to meet in the love of God. The complement to the ascetic side of marriage is gaining the social skills for life in the kingdom; if we are all members of one Body, perhaps marriage is the nearest (and that by some distance) earthly counterpart to the way we all will relate to each other in the full glow of his grace, which may incidentally be what Jesus meant about "neither marrying nor giving in marriage"—once I've received the message, I can hang up the telephone.

I sometimes wonder if purgatory is just heaven before we're used to it, and if so, whether marriage is part of the getting used to it. However that may be, Christian marriage does certainly aim at making each other's personhood in all its fullness totally real to ourselves, which will not happen when we see each other as mere devices towards our own comfort and convenience.

The Alienated Self

Marriage puts a spotlight on one who has lost the sense not only of the other as a person, but even of his own personhood. The literature on personality disorders in the last decade or so has been full of the way a dysfunctional family system can distort each of its members to fit its requirements at the expense of their own healthy growth and autonomy. Alcoholism, for example, is coming to be seen as a disease of the whole family, addict and enablers together, not just an isolated aberration in one individual. This kind of thing can take on a life of its own and pass from parent to child until someone manages to derail it: truly a case of the fathers' sins being visited on many generations. Clearly, one who is caught up in the ongoing falsehood can't relate to himself, much less anyone else.

In a culture full of such dysfunctional family systems constantly reacting on each other, as some say ours is, the chances of successful marriage are nil until grace is brought to bear on liberating souls from that quasi-possession. Here again, marriage issues reflect fundamental Church issues; salvation is liberation from the effects of the Big Lie we heard in the Garden and have carried with us ever since. We might say original sin means the whole human race is one big dysfunctional family waiting to be healed, and if so, then the sacrament of matrimony was created to bring the dysfunctional family in line with the Holy Family.

The Romantic Heresy

In any passing glance at the problems faced by today's Church, it should come high on the list that our liturgy seems to have lost its energy. The old liturgy depended on images, such as the agricultural cycle and the glory of an absolute monarch, that don't affect us as its originators had once intended. Our age knows rather too much about dictators and not enough about living close to the land. We find ourselves in the embarrassing position of losing the old magic without having any viable replacement in sight. This is a symptom of our scientistic age, with its quasi-religious compulsion to measure everything and to define its "everything" as "that which can be measured." It no longer recognizes its own deep thirst for the unmeasurable world of the spirit, for the very things we've carefully taught ourselves, culture-wide, to disdain. Nature will out, of course; enter the new mysticism to cater to our craving for ecstasy.

The spirit of our age offers its children the same old idolatry in every detail except the name of religion. We can have our gods and goddesses, our nymphs and satyrs, without the temples and the sacred groves (and with a good bit less decorum). We can go worship them any time at the nearest fern bar. The decline of our sense of the numinous in any visibly religious context coincides neatly with the rise of our culture's fascination with romantic love as the one and only true reason to enter a "meaningful relationship."

Anybody who seeks to do ministry in this field had better get straight on the difference between romantic love and "the Love that moves the sun and the other stars" (Dante, *Paradiso*, xxxiii). Confusion here is arguably the one greatest source of misery, disappointment, and blighted marriage active in today's western culture, not to mention near-ostracism for anyone who tries to meddle with this most sacred of popular idols, so it is worth pausing to consider for a moment.

Romantic love is fundamentally self-centered. It is all about my dreams, my desires, my ecstasy; the other is only the icon, in Jung's terms, for my own anima-projections. I never actually see the person I claim to love so passionately because the whole thing is going on only within my own psyche. When we say love is blind, we mean romantic love looks inward so intently it no longer perceives the objectified other as an independently existing entity. To speak of this as any kind of relationship is pure oxymoron. What we call failure in such a case is only the belated realization that we sought figs from thistles; that is, we have heaped impossible expectations on ourselves and each other, such that we'd be even more miserable if we ever actually got what we yearned for than we are when we can't have it.

When the bubble breaks, we consider ourselves abject failures. Worse, romantic love looks for a static, blissful happyever-after starting on the way down the church steps. That paves the way directly to the lament we hear so often: "Somehow we just grew apart. . . ." Well, of course we grew; life means growth, and the static bliss we dreamed of is another word for death.

Romantic love does not prepare us for the reality that life is all about cyclic processes, like heart-beat and breathing. We come together in love, so we grow; our growth allows us new encounters with each other and the new encounters lead to new growth. This need not surprise us when we recall the old insight about love as giving; growth equips us for new ways to exchange the gift of self, and the giving empowers the growth. Of course the process in both of its phases is messy and requires both courage and effort, neither of which are forthcoming from romance.

The love that does build a solid marriage is less dramatic; it promises less and, at first sight, demands less. It is the kind of love that changes the diapers and takes out the garbage. It is also the kind of love that quietly goes about creating a bond that will outlast anything that life can throw at it, the bond we hardly notice until we fall off life's trapeze and it catches us before we hit the ground, and bears us up on eagle's wings, as my favorite hymn puts it. This kind of love can heal the disorders noted above, that prevent us from relating to each other or ourselves.

Loss of vision, to recapitulate this point, and failure to get in touch with the other or with myself, and failure to understand what love is about, are the causes for failed marriage we see again and again in our ministry. Divorce ministers must study these issues thoroughly, including a rigorous self-evaluation, if they hope to do any good here at all. The reading list at the end of this manual is not there to be decorative!

A Note on Addiction

What is known as the addictive personality might well be considered an eighth capital sin, in the sense that it is a mode of being that insulates one from grace. It is also a major cause for failed marriages, for just that reason. Marriage is aimed at bringing us together in grace; addiction isolates us. This is true of all addictive modes: substance dependence (alcoholism) and process addiction (workaholism, cultism), active addiction and passive (codependency, the "enabler").

Addiction is a multi-person system, not an individual problem, and its effects are just as destructive whether or not the primary addict in the system is readily identifiable. A substance abuser, for instance, may turn out to be the enabler for a power addict. The phrase "She drove him to drink" can be the mere truth! This manual does not have space to examine the topic in sufficient detail but, since the estimates for the prevalence of addictive personality in this population, in one mode or another, range as high as 95 percent with great plausibility, it can be confidently expected that addiction will be a frequent and major issue in the ministry, and the minister will therefore need to study it thoroughly and, as usual, with earnest self-examination.

2

The Divorced Catholic and the Church

False Opinions about Divorce

Because so many of us are infected with the secular attitudes just described, it is hardly surprising that there are so many failed vocations among us, including marriage. Right after the sheer numbers of hurting souls, the biggest hassle and frustration the divorced Catholic and those who seek to minister to him or her will encounter is the mind-boggling variety of secularist superstitions and weird rumors we find floating around in the minds of our fellow parishioners, not excepting a sizable number of the clergy who surely ought to know better.

Why that should be is anybody's guess—perhaps some of us, confronted with pain, would rather confabulate than investigate—but the fact is that such superstitions present the divorce minister with formidable barriers to reaching out to those who need healing or to getting the well-meaning types pointed the right way. This is nothing unique; people who minister to AIDS or cancer patients or "challenged" persons will know what I'm saying. For example, some people believe that divorce means automatic excommunication, that divorced people are ineligible for public participation in the sacraments, that they aren't safe to have around, that they just didn't try hard enough (or that the Church is too lenient about demanding reconciliation), that years married or the presence of children mean annulments are impossible, etc.

We see pastors who simply refuse to deal with the issue, beyond what the bishop demands at gunpoint, because of such prejudices. We also see family members and so-called friends whose insensitivity and plain malice (thinly sugar-coated with the very best of stated intentions) make life miserable to the point of suicidal depression just when the person most needs a little kindness and support.

Persons doing divorce ministry must expect this sort of thing and allow for it in dealing with new clients; often the "Job's friends" have been even worse than the separation itself, in short-term pain inflicted, and the hurting person will be very reluctant to risk more of the same from us. They will often test us with assumed attitudes and side-issues before trusting us with their real troubles. Be prepared to see examples of aggressively held and expressed ignorance turning up every so often that beat anything your darkest imaginings would have thought possible.

Note that many divorced Catholics, having been scandalized by the very unchristian behavior of some professed Christians, will come to us displaying a lot of anger and hostility towards the institutional Church, including vehement anticlerical attitudes. They will seem almost to defy us, as Church people, to go ahead and just try to change their minds. This should be treated as seriously, and as literally, as a threat of suicide; that is, we are dealing with an especially deep and bitter pain and an especially urgent need for love. The Christlike thing to do is to concentrate on the broken heart first and lead them back to the institution later.

The Divorced Catholic's True Position

What is the true position of the divorced Catholic? First, she or he is in fact a bona fide Catholic of the very best possible standing, not only by absence of any cause for ostracism but because his or her need is a peremptory claim on our strenuous efforts to do whatever it takes to heal the pain and bring this person back to full and joyous functioning as a member of the Body of Christ. Nobody who cares about being a Christian will run out and get divorced just for kicks—most of us spend years agonizing over that decision, even when the grounds are self-evident, before anyone outside the family knows anything much is wrong. Not only that, but, as we will see, this person's experience can make him or her a valuable resource for the rest of us. A divorcing Catholic has an opportunity to join with Christ in "bearing the sins of the world" and to resemble him in being a "wounded healer" to the rest of us (Isaiah 53).

The Catholic's Experience of Divorce

The Grieving Process

Divorce is second only, if at all, to the death of a child or well-loved spouse as a personal disaster, and much the same grieving process applies. In the support group I lead, we have kicked this one around a number of times, and concluded that it is too close to call either way, even for the members who have been through both the death of one spouse and a divorce from another. Grief, as Elizabeth Kubler-Ross tells us so well in her writings on the subject, involves a series of fairly well defined steps that must be taken in proper sequence and at the necessary pace. It is a process, that is, as distinct from a one-shot event, and in ideal conditions may occupy as little as three to five years of reconstructive effort on the part of the person sustaining a loss of this magnitude. The divorce minister will want to study very closely her book or another like it and make its ideas his or her own before attempting to meddle with the grieving person in any depth.

Briefly, the stages of the grieving process according to Kubler-Ross are: Denial and Isolation, Anger, Bargaining, Depression, and Acceptance. Just as a person who suffers a traumatic physical injury will be in a state of shock at first, and not fully realize what has happened, a person's first response to severe emotional injury is likely to be *Denial*. Bad news just takes time to sink in (note this is not the same "denial" that figures in discussions of addiction). Analogous to the arrival of physical pain when the shock wears off is the stage of *Anger*, in which one is quite properly outraged at the cosmic obscenity that has exploded into one's life, and naturally expresses this outrage to God, to the human perpetrators, and to anything else that moves. Then comes the *Bargaining* phase, in which one looks for ways to escape or mitigate the situation, like an accident victim seeking a more comfortable or at least less painful position. When that proves futile, one enters *Depression*, in which the anger turns inward and one feels not only dejected at one's lot but guilty and inadequate about one's failure to meet one's own expectations and perceived responsibilities to others, and about one's dreams that will now never come true. Finally, as one finishes processing through all that, one enters the *Acceptance* phase in which, if not yet happy or at peace, one at least begins to move on from the past disaster and get on with whatever is coming next. Note that the whole process applies not only to the person directly affected by death or divorce, but also to those closely involved: family, close friends, and ministers; divorce ministry, while rewarding, can also be emotionally expensive—make sure you have your own support system in place!

Unfinished Business

Divorce inevitably brings to the surface, like a bomb in a graveyard, all manner of buried issues from the past: all the unfinished business from childhood as well as from the marriage itself (which often has recapitulated the earlier material). This can be the opportunity of a lifetime for this person to confront those issues and deal with them in a healing way. The process can get hairy when—as happens far more often than one might have expected—those issues have to do with family alcoholism, child abuse, incest, and the like. Those who have not encountered this before will be horrified at how pervasive this kind of thing is, and how vile some parents or others can be in their treatment of children.

Even without such a horror story, failed marriages are very often the latest step in a trail that leads plainly and directly back to a dysfunctional home. We're not talking about some subtle deduction by a psychoanalyst; this is stuff even the person involved can see clearly without prompting. Likewise, it does not require the divorce minister to be a mental health professional; in fact, divorce ministry other than formal psychiatric practice should vigorously dissociate itself from any suggestion that we do any kind of mental health therapy per se— there are liabilities here that we need to steer well clear of. Our practice is only to empower and affirm the hurting person's self-healing process. The purpose in educating ourselves about this area is to know what pitfalls to avoid and perhaps administer a bit of emotional first-aid until the client can hook up with a therapist, if that is appropriate.

Brave New World

The other side of the coin from the unfinished business is that the chaotic new world that reveals itself to the newly divorced person after some of the dust has settled represents an opportunity to rebuild in any way she or he chooses. This freedom is normally very distressing at first; the risks are much more visible than the opportunities, and one's first reaction is likely to be sheer panic and a retreat to the fetal position. We see a lot of infantile acting-out at this point, and it is vital to bear in mind that this is a normal and (up to a point) desirable stage in the healing process. The one thing we are not called upon to do here is sit in judgment by the standards we would apply to someone in better circumstances.

Crisis of Faith

Divorce for a seriously believing Catholic is an outrage of truly cosmic proportions. The stability of a sacramental marriage is one of those supposed eternal verities that support everything else, and when one's marriage fails, one begins to wonder if the rest of life also is just a big practical joke played on us by a malevolent God. How else explain this mess, if I haven't been played for a sucker in the one area, my faith, where I'd always believed I was safest? Now I know what Job was about! And so on . . . . This is when a person typically becomes extra sensitive to the many changes we have seen in the last generation. For example, the number of new vocations to the priesthood and religious life is falling, and as the existing priests and religious retire or return to lay life, many of their traditional functions are defaulting back to lay persons. Church functions that used to be a clerical male monopoly are increasingly peformed by women. These things have led us to reconsider the distinctions between the natures of the priesthood per se and of ministry in general.

Similarly, the up-for-grabs moral climate of our secular society has led to earnest reexamination of our ethics and of the whole normative process: how does the Church's *magisterium* coexist with one's personal conscience and the responsibility that goes with it? Put another way, just what is an active Catholic? Is there such a thing as a passive Catholic? In the secular world, the melee among pop-science, secular humanism, sectarianism, and the challenges to (and by) civil authority reflect a deep sense of unease about fundamental questions that turns up in many people's religious experience as well, often in the form of the alienation so vividly described in books like Toffler's *Future Shock* or Morris's *Human Zoo*, which consider the effects of constant, rapid change and of sheer population density, respectively, on our society and ourselves.

Or again: the form and function of our liturgy have engendered heated controversy while Mass attendance plummets, and those who still show up in church often complain that the "liturgical fidgets" have robbed the Mass of its emotive power, so that we have lost the mythic and emotional foundations that used to support much of our conscious identity as Catholics, with little apparent gain in return. Finally, money problems that were always troublesome enough before have now led to the closing and consolidation of parishes, to the dismay of parishioners who wonder how we can have a Church at all without the familiar, traditional parish structure.

The divorced Catholic will often be deeply troubled by all this and by real or perceived affronts by fellow Catholics, especially clergy, and s/he will express that disturbance in no very temperate terms. This too is part of the healing, and if we hear people ventilating certain theological propositions that differ from what we normally hear on a Sunday morning, we are probably more offended than God is. He's been there himself—". . . why have you abandoned me?"—and we, again, are called upon to bear silent witness that God does care, and hasn't really gone anywhere, that being why we're there; the emphasis here is on the word "silent."

Reconciliation is not possible until we have acknowledged properly that which needs to be reconciled. In divorce, one is alienated from oneself, from one's spouse, from other significant persons, from our social environment, from the institutional Church, and from God, all at once. One needs to find ways to reconciliation in all these relationships, also all at once. This is a very painful situation to be in. The main cure is simply the passage of time in a supportive environment that allows the hurting person space to fit the pieces together. Eventually, the hurting person will gain enough insight to entertain the notion that forgiveness of and by each of us is the central Christian experience, which should grow outwards from one's own salvation experience to all the other relationships just mentioned. Forgiveness means full acknowledgement of what went wrong, in order to heal it in oneself and (if possible) in the other. That is straightforward enough to read in a book; making it one's own in the midst of suffering is something else again.

Lawyers

I do not personally know of anyone who has been through a divorce and still has anything like a positive feeling for lawyers. The unfortunate reality is that the legal system is still set up to make its practitioners rich at the expense of everyone else's personal tragedies. All too often we see such practitioners aggravate the divorcing couple's conflicts, taking deliberate advantage of their temporarily vulnerable mental state, in order to bill for yet more pointless activity.

Those whose practice is an exception to that trend only serve to emphasize it by their scarcity. I do not say this lightly; it is the overwhelming consensus every time the subject comes up in every group I've ever met with, which by now amounts to a sizable cross section of our population. Be prepared to encounter a roomful of extremely bitter people when, as you should occasionally, you hold a session on legal issues. The hurt will be second, by a narrow margin, only to that received from those unworthy shepherds we discussed earlier.

While we can do little, in the short term, to clean up the court system, we should be aware of ways to minimize its harmful effects and of certain positive trends presently underway within the field itself. There is a huge market opportunity here for Catholic attorneys who care to make their profession a form of ministry; in many states there is a movement in attitude away from adversarial confrontation to some concern for the true well-being of the children and the separating spouses (e.g., in encouraging the spouses to settle their affairs in mediation instead of by litigation). The Catholic family law specialist, mindful of his responsibilities before God, has an opportunity rare in his profession to be not only moral but fashionable. Encouragement of such an approach, for example through a diocesan "St. Thomas More Guild," should be a high priority everywhere.

We in California strongly recommend the legal resources provided by Nolo Press in Berkeley. They put out, among many other nifty things, a book on how to do one's own California dissolution, which they update every year to reflect changes in the family law code. This does not always dispense one from needing an attorney, but it does spell out the issues involved and the way the code attempts to address those issues. This provides a great antidote to both the curbstone lawyers among one's friends and the unscrupulous esquires noted above; if both spouses read it intelligently, life tends to get a lot better in a hurry. Since family law varies widely from state to state, you will need to shop around for an equivalent, if any, where you live—another market gap, perhaps, for the Catholic family law specialist.

Gender Issues

It is impossible to say anything about gender, or even mention it, without offending someone. Nevertheless the issue is as real as it is volatile, and it must be addressed.

The feminists have rightly challenged the widespread, deep-seated legal, societal, and ecclesial presumptions of women's inferiority in our culture. In so doing, they have raised questions for men, as well, about the kind of maleness that had been presumed superior and the distortions and penalties it had brought for the majority of real-world men as well as for women. Women can rightly demand proper recognition of their human dignity; men likewise can rightly demand greater realism—indeed, mere sanity!—in society's expectations of them.

Our all-too-human legal system is stuck right in the middle for a whole range of questions, such as what is fair spousal support and how to assign child custody, in which it is ill-equipped to satisfy anyone in the real world, so that both men and women, in different ways, have gotten a raw deal throughout the divorce process. Each then tends to blame the other, both in general and as personified by the ex-spouse, and in fact to incur such blame by anticipating the injuries the other is stereotypically expected to inflict. The extra and quite unnecessary suffering this causes is incalculable. We have seen much healing in groups where both are well represented and encouraged to speak out honestly and thoughtfully. In this, we owe a great debt to the trend in some feminist circles to see that our culture's attitude to women is inseparable from its corresponding distortion of men, and that the way to advance themselves is to heal both.

While there is great benefit in bringing both genders together in the support group, it is useful to provide groups devoted to men's issues as well for those interested, in particular for opting out of the macho, "big boys don't cry" stereotype. Even allowing for the trend that men remarry sooner, our groups attract disproportionately fewer men, which is nothing short of tragic. I have no ready answer for this problem, but some solution is badly needed. Let me know, via The Liturgical Press, if something works well for you, and we'll include it in the next edition.

Divorcee's Dementia

Added to all that, the newly divorced person will experience all the symptoms of any other major upheaval in life: mood swings, odd impulses, depression, a general inability to keep any structure to one's practical affairs such as keeping the checkbook balanced or the bills paid when they could be, a dazed, unfocused response to life, and alienation of most of one's friends in consequence of an irresistible need to talk about it all, in season and (mostly) out. If you haven't been through this yourself, you really can't know just how goofy a person can get, or how hopelessly lost. Nor does it help much to be what is loosely known as "a good Catholic." This experience temporarily knocks all that into a cocked hat, and the sudden derangement of one's former security in the faith is the most demoralizing part of the whole mess. This is not the time for a bracing discourse on trust in the Lord, nor for an exhortation to "just pull yourself together!" In fact, this is not the time for much of anything except an absorbent shoulder and an available ear.

A Digression on Anger

We often see people who are troubled about their own anger; we were brought up to believe such emotions aren't nice. Unfortunately, some shepherds of souls still think so, and advise their patients that anger is a sin, or something very like, and must be resisted. This can lead to serious harm, including physical disease and accident proneness. A more enlightened approach is that anger is the emotional equivalent of physical pain (which we are also, too often, taught to ignore and deny) and, as such, is a vitally important cue to us to check and see what is wrong, and motivates us to correct the situation. Or we can say it is like the fever that shows one's body is fighting an infection.

3

The Divorce Minister's Toolkit

From our discussion of the traumas and troubles faced by the divorced person, the fundamentals of ministry should be fairly self evident by now. Divorce ministry, given the roughly 50 percent marital failure rate we see at present, is for everyone across the board, from local Ordinary to casual neighbor. It breaks down to three main components: education before the event, supportive listening after, and practical assistance in cleaning up the mess.

Premarital Catechesis

With the greatest of respect for our hardworking catechists and reverence for their zeal for the Lord (and I paid my dues here for some years myself), the divorce statistics, the Tribunal caseload, and the percentage of cases that result in a decree of nullity represent a massive failure in our past efforts to educate our children and young adults about the realities of Christian marriage. In effect, we have abandoned the field to Hollywood, to the advertizing industry, to the popular songwriters, and to the secular world's porno-romantic fantasies, all of which have so thoroughly corrupted our ability to hear and understand the Gospel viewpoint that a discussion such as this may well have some difficulty obtaining a hearing even among supposedly well-informed, committed Catholics.

This is not a new problem. In the past, marriages appeared to stay together because the weight of social sanction was against admitting failure and because women had few recourses after separation. The resulting suffering was horrendous. Our present statistics merely reflect more honestly what was already there. What is new is the secular world's acceptance of divorce; our catechetic ailment has been with us for a very long time, as the overwhelming weight of testimony in our groups has convinced us. Today's divorcees are working through their great grandparents' heartaches. The same is true, of course, of the crisis in vocations generally.

Those of us who are parents should see a serious responsibility here, starting as soon as a child can talk. Members of parent-teacher organizations might well ask some pointed questions about what is being taught about this at their school and with what emphasis (just before Valentine's Day, for instance). Nor should we forget the CCD program. Members of parish councils might do likewise. The poor catechesis has existed for no better reason than that those of us who knew better sat back and did nothing about it. It is amazing how much influence on curricula is exercised by default!

The same holds true of the local marriage preparation program, if any (and if there is none, why not?). It still happens that some good-ole-boy pastors will perform a church wedding for any stray couple that asks, regardless of all the failures and all the bishops' edicts to the contrary. In view of the harm that does, we need feel no hesitation about turning on the lights for the bishop to see—that's our Church they're damaging.

Let me repeat: many of us have worked heroically hard and long to provide our young people with a Christian education. It would be beastly of me to fault either the effort or the good-will. But the visible results simply don't square with the effort, no matter what we may feel about that undeniable fact. I meet with my evidence twice a month and spend some hours between times doing crisis intervention besides, undoing the results of lifetimes of inadequate catechesis. As for revitalizing the content of that education, we have two excellent resources in the tribunal and in our recovering divorced persons themselves—if we take the trouble to consult them.

Postmarital Support

Marriage Encounter is already doing excellent work in many places, but the field is woefully short of workers. We believe a significant proportion of troubled Catholic marriages could be saved if the couple had somewhere to turn; if they don't know about it, or if it is not presented in terms of their perceived needs, it doesn't exist for them. Support systems for the still-married need to exercise some creative entrepeneurship here, starting from the unfortunate fact that couples who need them the most are often least likely to take the initiative in meeting their own needs.

Retrouvaille is another excellent organization with a program for bringing troubled marriages together before it is too late. Its format is a retreat style weekend followed by a series of weekly meetings, designed to get a couple communicating in constructive ways.

Divorce ministry must work closely with such programs; the sooner that puts us out of business, the better!

Post Separation Assistance

The North American Conference of Separated and Divorced Catholics

Given the fact of separation, everyone who encounters the separated person becomes a minister of one kind or another. We are all responsible for how we bear our roles as representatives of the Christian community to each of our neighbors ("Whatever you do . . .").

Some years ago, some of us who were ourselves divorced and Catholic recognized that fact and realized, further, that if we did not come together to help ourselves, nobody else was going to do it for us. The result was an organization called the North American Conference of Separated and Divorced Catholics (NACSDC). After some adventurous early years, NACSDC is now one of the largest Catholic lay organizations in English-speaking North America, with several thousand small support groups at work in dioceses across the continent. The organization is divided in regions, to correspond with the regional bishops' conferences, and within each region we are usually affiliated with the diocesan family life office or equivalent. The small groups are, by preference, set up as parish organizations, but some are attached to college campuses or otherwise as seems appropriate.

The essential ministry of NACSDC is through the small groups, but these are supplemented with other activities, such as short-term divorce-adjustment programs for the newly-separated (typically seven consecutive weeks—see below), regional and national annual conferences, a large catalog of literature, including an excellent magazine called *Jacob's Well* in honor of the divorced woman Jesus met there, and increasing recognition as an advisory resource for the bishops' efforts to address our marital crisis. While affiliation with NACSDC is not absolutely essential to effective divorce ministry, nonaffiliation is really doing it the hard way, not only because the resources are already there but because of the fellowship with thousands of others in the same field. Any ministry can get lonely, and this one in particular; it is hard to exaggerate how good it can be to work in unity with others.

Essence of Effective Ministry: LISTENING

For most of us, ministry in whatever mode consists simply of listening and of staying put when the separated person needs someone around. Advice is beside the point; we are not called upon to say the right thing, or to say anything at all. Just pressing the hand without words and letting the hurting person read between the lines is usually enough. For the hurting person the important thing is the comfort and affirmation in being heard and taken seriously; the healing itself comes through the self-expression, and any advances in insight will come the same way, from within. Trying to tell this person my own understanding is like addressing someone's hunger by making them watch me eat; for the understanding to do any good, it must be one's own, reached for oneself.

Unless you are a mental health professional, it is best to leave it at that. Well-intentioned meddling by persons without professional qualifications can do a great deal of harm to the already hurting person, not to mention the potential for a variety of legal headaches for the would-be minister. This applies even (especially) when the person asks for advice or guidance, as hurting people often do. The answer then is either "I don't know," which is always the truth since one's insight applies to oneself only, or something like "What do you think?" to get the person talking again.

While we encourage people to talk out their stories, we must never probe or otherwise try to hurry them out of their own natural pace. The point is for them to have the experience of telling their own stories in their own way, not for us to know the stories to the gratification of our own curiosity. Getting someone unstuck is another matter: the example of the others' sharing, combined with a gentle and nonjudgmental invitation to follow suit, will in time do the job.

Beware above all the temptation, and examine your conscience rigorously and often for any trace of it, to be at all impressed with your own advanced insight and exalted spirituality; therein lies the nearest way to making yourself the most egregious fool in Christendom (experience speaks . . .). Even in the unlikely event that one really is something special, that would be totally irrelevant to the task at hand. The etymology of "humility" has to do with one's feet being on the ground: see that they stay there!

Note that, in keeping with our insights about the new divorcee's sense of powerlessness, we can give a renewed sense of empowerment by things like asking permission to visit, to hear the story, or to help in some other way. Even a small detail like, "*May* I sit with you a while?" can make a big difference.

The Small Support Group—The Backbone of Divorce Ministry

The primary method of ministry to divorced persons is the small group. By this we do not mean a confrontational encounter group, nor a singles "meet market," nor a lecture assembly. It is not something handed down from the official Church ready-made, nor is it prescriptive therapy done by persons not themselves affected by the problems in question. Members of the divorce support group attend to do two things: first, to tell their own stories in a caring, affirming environment; and second, to listen to the stories of others as they wish themselves to be heard. That is to say, this is a peer ministry, conducted by the persons themselves who need it, to each other. The essence of small group ministry here is mutual empowerment through mutual support, mutual listening, and mutual affirmation. It is impossible to exaggerate the importance of that point or the absolute necessity of holding to it in all its simplicity.

STAGES OF RECOVERY FOR GROUP MEMBERS

Group members can be at any point in the recovery process and both gain from the group and contribute to it. For purposes of this discussion, we can speak of three major phases in recovery: Crisis, Convalescence, and Consolidation.

In the *Crisis* phase one is disoriented, in a state of shock, angry, depressed, cynical, alienated from everyone and everything, and above all, thoroughly hurting. The task here is just to hang on and avoid doing anything permanently regrettable until the bleeding stops and the pain recedes enough to begin functioning again. In this phase, ministry consists of pure listening, as described above.

In the *Convalescence* phase one begins to get one's bearings and take some interest in life and to start to do something constructive about the problems both internal (coping with anger and so on) and external (the legal mess, money, where to live). It is usually very helpful at this point to compare notes with others in the same situation and exchange encouragement; this is also the time to offer information about the issues of interest (but not advice). The group might have guest speakers occasionally to discuss the issues, then open the floor for a rap session.

In the *Consolidation* phase things are beginning to fall into place and the main issue, paradoxically, is how to adjust to life's being good again. One's self esteem begins to return and, after its long absence, this can be a bit unsettling at first. This phase is rather like the physical therapy after the cast is off. Persons in each phase have something to offer and something to gain from people in the other phases; the interrelationships must be seen as horizontal rather than vertical, on the model of 1 Corinthians 12.

Pitfalls

The route through these phases from catastrophe to healing has some pitfalls among the opportunities. We often see someone get stuck at some point, either for lack of insight or for fear of letting go of what is familiar, however miserable it is. Such people have what we call the "shoe-nailed-to-the-floor" syndrome; they tend to go round and round on the same groove on the same broken record meeting after meeting, and whatever anyone else says reminds them of that one theme. It is normal to repeat one's story many times, but over several meetings we should see some movement, some shift in emphasis as the member slowly processes through his or her case. Where there is no movement over a couple of months, we may need to prod a little, or suggest time out with a therapist, in order to avoid disrupting the other members.

Another mode of getting stuck and copping-out on the recovery process is the tendency some members have of slipping into the "we-precious-few" mentality, in which belonging to the charmed circle (and excluding others) comes to outweigh personal growth or ministry to others. The cure will depend on some discretion here, whether it is better to let the clique drift away into its own little world or try to wake them up and retrieve them. Again, the main consideration is the well-being of the rest of the group.

The most common variant of the inner circle syndrome is a leadership style that centers on the leaders' own immediate needs exclusively in matters such as the selection of meeting themes. This can be as insidious as it is harmful. A similar problem is the politicians who try to use the group to display their own prestige. This should not be too much of a problem in a peer ministry group where the service is all horizontal, but it does happen sometimes. The best cure is prevention: keep the leadership functions so minimal as not to attract the ego-tripper.

Our biggest problem in actual practice has been the "cuckoo-in-the-nest" types who come in with their own, other agendas and try to co-opt the support group instead of starting their own groups from scratch. This can be especially troublesome when the extraneous purpose is similar enough to be plausible. Examples are the singles who want to set up a meet market, which is directly contrary to the essence of our ministry, and persons such as the widowed who want to conduct their own therapy without hearing about divorce issues. This can call for some diplomacy, since a single person might legitimately want to get some benefit from our experience before taking his or her own plunge (which is one of the spin-offs we can offer to the community at large). A widow(er) has many of the same issues to process, and our groups do commonly include such people without difficulty. It can be a very fine line to steer between accommodation and subversion.

STARTING THE SMALL SUPPORT GROUP

As will by now be apparent, starting and organizing a small group of this kind is different from most Church activities. The initiative cannot begin with the local rectory, although, once started, it will benefit immensely from the pastor's encouragement. The initial impulse to begin must come from the prospective members themselves, either when several discover each other's presence in the community and start to talk among themselves, or when some other activity creates favorable conditions. This point is absolutely essential; any attempt to bypass it will defeat the group before it starts. At the same time, of course, it makes no sense to attempt to start a group as a parish organization when the pastor is unwilling to support it, as happens, unfortunately. Persons starting a group should find a sympathetic pastor and keep him informed of what they are doing, even though they do not directly involve him until later. Methods we have found helpful include the following (but do by all means use your creativity in addressing your own community):

• A short-term program such as the "seven weeks" described below; if the attendees come from the same area and have achieved a useful sense of community with each other, the impulse to continue as a support group will be automatic.

• Regional conferences such as those conducted by NACSDC are a natural forum for recruiting.

• Distribution of appropriate literature such as the extensive list carried by NACSDC and other organizations (or this manual) can sometimes, in the right hands, move people to start something (but don't bet on it apart from other efforts).

• It is possible for the pastor to prompt a gathering of some of the divorcing people who come to him for help, or (preferably) direct them to a preparatory activity such as the seven weeks program, as long as it is clear they are expected to do their own ministry. It is better if the divorced persons get together, first, among themselves and then approach the pastor for support and perhaps a place to meet. Or on a Sunday when the gospel is germane, the founders of the new group could address the congregation with a brief announcement about the nature and meeting times of the group. Once the group is properly started, of course, the pastor can refer new people to it as a routine adjunct to his own ministry.

• Groups with related goals or with members likely to need our services may be willing to cooperate with us in directing applicants to one or the other. This is especially true of the twelve-step programs such as AA, Alanon, or ACOA, whose members include a very high proportion of divorced persons, just as our groups will likely include candidates for the twelve-step programs. The affinity here is not accidental, since recovery from divorce has a lot in common with recovery from substance or process abuse or from codependency, and the NACSDC small group is loosely modeled on the AA format.

The divorce minister will need to investigate the set of issues surrounding addiction since these will constantly come up in dealing with divorced persons; it would be an excellent idea to get a copy of the AA "Blue Book" and study it closely. It is also highly advisable to seek out the leaders of whichever twelve-step groups exist locally and construct a good working relationship with them for mutual referrals and the like. Do not overlook the divorce ministries of other faiths, nor their secular counterparts.

The Meeting

Meeting formats should be kept rather loose, while at the same time keeping to a clear purpose. Typically, a meeting will start promptly on time (remember, single parents will need to get home on schedule) with a brief prayer or reading and some sort of introduction around the room ("My name is _____, I've been separated _____ months, I'm here to . . ."). A member or guest might give a half hour or so presentation on some topic of interest, then open the discussion to members' participation.

Each member should have a chance, but not be compelled, to speak her or his piece. This is not a business meeting; if a member feels a need to depart from the evening's topic in favor of something more personally urgent, she or he is entitled to be heard attentively and with respect. It should go without saying, but unfortunately does sometimes need saying, that whatever happens in the meeting must stay there; the member must feel absolutely confident that his or her story will not be gossipped about anywhere else.

The presider, who might or might not be the group leader, should begin to wrap things up with announcements and a brief dispatch of any business matters about a half hour before the meeting is scheduled to end, so that the members will have a chance to socialize over coffee and cookies or whatever before leaving.

In particular, do not let the meeting break up before passing the kitty! Dues are important for small incidentals like postage and coffee. I'm rather taken with the way this is handled by the Legion of Mary, which in order to avoid drawing notice to different members' different abilities to contribute passes the "secret bag," which is a sack or other narrow mouthed container into which one either puts what seems right or discreetly gives a snap of the thumb to make it rattle. Besides avoiding embarrassment, this is just the kind of quirky custom that builds esprit de corps.

Presentation and discussion topics should be chosen and publicized well in advance, to give people a chance to plan on attending meetings of particular interest. Topics should be directly related to the members' current experiences and problems, such as legal issues, money, adjusting to single life, child care, emotional issues (anger, guilt, disorientation), one's place in the Church, and so on. It is a good idea to have at least a general plan for the cycle of topics over the year, to address matters of seasonal interest or major events such as the local conference. Planning the agenda for the next few months is a good way to involve new people in the core group, by the way. Two or three times a year, minimum, there should be a purely social activity (e.g., a Christmas party) for the members to relax and have some fun and build friendships in a safe, nonmatchmaking context. This is especially important around the end of the year, when newly-lonely people are vulnerable to serious depression.

ORGANIZATION

Organization can be a difficult issue, in that the need to ensure the orderly continuation of the group can conflict with a newly divorced person's normal inability to plan or commit very far in advance. There are probably as many theories about this as there are organizers; what follows has worked for us in our specific local context. Feel free to tinker with improvements after you've tried it for a while.

The hierarchical arrangement we see in most groups, by which members commit to long term roles with clear-cut functions, is not well suited here, since hurting people are not well known for their ability to make a commitment beyond tomorrow morning or to undertake significant new responsibilities. Furthermore, the healing goal, which takes precedence over all other considerations, can be very effectively addressed by encouraging members to undertake small, readily achieved tasks, such as bringing next week's refreshments, where a larger responsibility would scare them away.

For these reasons, we discourage elaborate rules and long lists of "officers." It is far more effective, if a bit untidy, to keep the designated officialities to a bare minimum: a leader, whose functions are to provide a phone number as contact person for the group, to conduct meetings, and to encourage participation by newer members, and a treasurer, whose function is to keep the bank happy in matters like authorized signatures for the group's account, which should be deliberately kept small.

Leadership, in the conventional sense, is exercised by a more amorphous core group, made up of whichever members are available and willing to plan meetings, set up furniture, run the telephone tree, etc. Members of the core group are selected by their happening to be present when something needs to be done or decided, according to their abilities and interests. They can be at any point in the recovery cycle, and their contributions should be measured by what they can handle. For a person in the crisis phase, getting the agenda photocopied can be a major accomplishment, to be recognized publicly as such; for someone in consolidation phase, setting up a social event might be readily taken in stride but should still be recognized and appreciated.

A subtle but very important consideration here is how the nature of the leadership determines the effectiveness of the group. If it caters to a set of people, it will die when they move on, because new members will not be attracted. If it caters to a set of needs, there will be more turnover but the group itself will last longer. The ideal is to keep a good balance among the different sets of needs discussed above under "Stages of Recovery," so that new people keep coming in but a core group of ministers will stay around longer. It is vital to include new members in decision making as soon as they join.

The more adventurous might consider a scheme based on the "Power Cycle" I've seen discussed by some feminist groups as a way to avoid the hierarchical model. It works like this: Suppose I'm walking down the street and stub my toe. I do a double-take, change course slightly, and keep on walking.

My progress down the street is a series of such interactions with my surroundings, guided by my overall purpose (if any) in walking.

We might diagram the cycle:

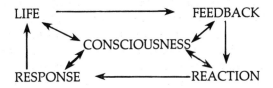

where LIFE corresponds to walking down the street, FEEDBACK to the stubbed toe, REACTION to the double-take, and RESPONSE to walking around the obstacle. We can depict the same cycle for an organization like this:

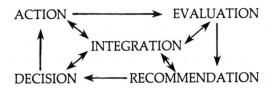

In any group some members are better endowed for some of these functions than for others. Traditionally, the DECISION specialist has been what we've called the leader; the EVALUATOR has been his disruptive antagonist, the RECOMMENDOR has been the dreamer, and the ACTOR has done the work. This has been so because we have accepted hierarchy, with its surrender and delegation of powers, as the price of structure and order.

We can also route our power structure horizontally, not vertically. In such a model, leadership, so far as it is visible at all, rests with the INTEGRATOR (think of Ben Franklin at the Constitutional Convention). It consists of bringing together a combination of talents suited to the question of the moment and letting the group chemistry do the work. Instead of electing people to fill offices, such a scheme operates by a running match between the shopping list of things to get done and the row of people available at the moment.

While messy, this has several important advantages: the group can't be paralyzed by the absence of any "key" person; status games are minimized; work load is spread throughout the group (no idle passengers); talents and contributions can be more evenly used and appreciated; long term commitments are less critical; and each member's personal growth, empowerment, and self-esteem—the point to the whole exercise—are maximized without anyone's being overwhelmed by the group's demands. Of course, this will require a lot of faith in one's fellow members, and the justification for that faith may not always make itself obvious in the short term. This is where we need to reflect upon the fact that we are after all doing Christian ministry specifically as such, meaning the true leader cannot be one or the other human member, however wise, but must be the Holy Spirit without whom we'd best have stayed at home anyway. If the Spirit wants a thing to happen, it will happen even in spite of me; if not, so it goes.

Advisory Board

Much the same applies beyond the small group itself. In our archdiocese a group leaders' group sprang up in the course of a party a few years ago for the dual purpose of liaison among the groups and other participants in the ministry such as the local Beginning Experience (BE) team, and of nurturing the nurturers. As it now stands, membership consists of anyone who feels the need or can contribute something to the bimonthly meetings, and the functions are to serve as an advisory board for the ministry, to publish a monthly newsletter containing a calendar of events, announcements, and an editorial page, to coordinate archdiocesan events, and to stave off ministers' burnout by spreading the load and by first-aid therapizing. As described above, we have been successful in keeping the formalities to a minimum and thereby eliminating harmful politics and in maintaining continuity through the normal high turnover rate in membership. Of course this keeps our integrators hopping! This is our own development, and your diocese will most likely have a different arrangement; no standard has yet emerged.

The Divorce Adjustment Program

The Divorce Adjustment Program is a series of meetings for newly divorced persons, aimed at providing them with a toolkit for dealing with the process of recovery. The format is something like a small support group except for being more structured and directed by the facilitation team. There are many different local programs of this type, including some that are modelled on the twelve-step format to the extent of running for twelve weeks instead of our more usual seven, and the device is also popular among some nonaffiliated mental health professionals. We find seven weeks a workable compromise between the length of time we can reasonably expect people to commit to, and the amount of material that needs to be covered. The format I have been trained for and used with success uses these topics for the seven weeks:

1. Admitting and accepting the fact that I am Catholic and divorced.
2. Realizing I am neither alone nor abnormal nor abandoned by the Christian community.
3. Sorting out my relationship with God in my new way of life.
4. Healing and forgiveness.

5. Letting go of the past and moving on in the present, including past and present ways of dealing with my nature as a sexual being.
6. Dealing with the process of change and growth.
7. Integrating my experience with the reality that mutual ministry is the constant fundamental principle of Christian community life.

The facilitators conduct the meeting by alternating their own modeling of the recovery process with ample opportunity for the participants to tell their own stories and compare notes but not exchange advice as such—everybody's road is different. The object is not to provide set answers to life's problems but to model an effective approach to solving those problems for oneself and to empower the newly divorced person in so doing. A group should be limited to between eight and twelve or so participants with, ideally, four facilitators; we run ours with a priest, a nun (who happens to be the divorce ministry coordinator for our archdiocese), a lay woman, and a lay man. Our thinking is that in this way we provide access to both genders of both states of life, which should mean the participant has at least one person present to approach comfortably. From one week to another we take turns leading the meeting and doing the other functions within meetings, such as introducing the evening's topic, leading subgroups if we divide into such for discussion, or leading closing prayers.

We purposely avoid planning the details of our meetings too tightly in advance so that we can adapt ourselves to the chemistry of the group as we go along. Our experience has typically been that the group begins bonding together by the second week and doing our work for us around the fourth week; the exhilaration for ourselves and for the participants has to be experienced—I can't describe the joy of seeing broken people begin to mend as we watch. By the last week, which closes with celebration of the Eucharist and a quiet potluck party, the group is looking for ways to continue meeting, and we have the core for a new support group or an infusion to the existing groups in the area.

Of course, there is more to this than just getting a few people together. It requires a lot of preparation and a lot of marketing among the local clergy on whom we depend for referrals. The same considerations apply here as for conference publicity, as described below, especially the year-round marketing presence that lends effect to attempts to publicize specific events. The payoff for the parish staffs in the area is that our program handles a lot of issues in the group that they would otherwise have to handle for individuals one by one, allowing more efficient and effective use of their time. It also often leads to recruitment of new and highly motivated parish workers.

The mental barriers we have encountered in selling this idea have been the attitude, noted above, that rejects the whole idea of divorce ministry without looking at it, and the fear that we are yet another program to add to the already ridiculous burden laid on the resources of the parish and its staff (which is one reason we insist on being a self-supporting lay peer-ministry).

It is very important that prospective members be screened before the series begins; this program is not for everyone. The emotional energy flying about can get very intense, and some people can't handle it. Also, a severely dysfunctional personality can disrupt it for everyone else. We suggest that persons who are seeing mental health professionals should sign a release form and have the counselor contact us to discuss the suitability of the program.

We earnestly recommend charging significantly for this program. Its success depends on each member's faithful attendance and participation which, in our experience, don't come for free. In 1989, we find between $40 and $80 per person is reasonable; for sixty facilitators' person-hours plus planning, preparation, materials, and the meeting place, this compares well with the going rate of $150 or so for a weekend retreat. In cases where a person truly cannot afford that rate, we can always negotiate some accommodation or even a freebie, provided we stress that someone else is carrying his/her expenses.

A further consideration is that staffing the program with lay facilitators involves finding and training people who are far enough along in their own recovery process both to do well at it and to benefit from it themselves. In other words, it is mutual ministry at work again, in which my ministry is also my therapy and my preparation to graduate into the ministering community at large.

The Regional Conference

While running the regional conference is a function of the NACSDC staff as such, it is useful for persons doing other forms of divorce ministry to know what it is and how to profit from it. Of course there is no reason why a local ministry couldn't do their own conference as well, and many do. A typical conference is a one-day gathering of separated and divorced persons for a series of workshops and other activities, with much the same purposes as the seven weeks program.

In our region that means a 9:00 a.m. assembly for orientation and keynote address, a morning workshop, lunch break, two afternoon workshops, Mass, and winding-down social (some years we include dinner). The workshops are an hour and a half each, and each person attending can choose three out of a list of eighteen or so. Topics range over the issues of interest to divorced people, from legal issues to sexuality to how to handle holidays to single parenting to annulments to remarriage and step-parenting.

We have at least one local Catholic bookstore represented with a literature table, as well as any other organizations in the area such as Beginning Experience (see below) whose activities harmonize with ours. All that makes for a very intense day with a lot of psychic energy flying about, so we do the conference on a Saturday and warn our attendees to plan for a very quiet Sunday to recover.

Lest one think having several hundred divorced people all in one place might be a bit dismal, rest assured it is all the other way. I've never participated in a more uplifting, energizing occasion than the conferences I've attended and staffed. Apparently others feel the same way; every conference I've attended led several people back to the sacraments after being away as long as twenty years and more, without explicitly exhorting them to do so.

A local ministry attempting to do a conference for the first time will do well to consult with their NACSDC region staff for advice. Our region begins planning its annual conference immediately after the previous one has ended; not only do we need to collect workers, but the facilities book that far in advance, and the people who do the workshops also tend to have full schedules. We usually rent space in a Catholic high school, which has the required classrooms, auditorium/chapel, and cafeteria and related facilities.

We typically experience some anxiety about attendance, since the facilities are expensive and we never know until the day itself how many people will show up, and therefore whether we will break even or not. Preregistration in our area is seldom more than three-fifths or so of the final total (divorced people, again, are not famous for planning ahead). This can create headaches, especially the first few times, when deciding what to charge the attendees. By the way, do charge for this—it ensures some motivation to show up and take things seriously. We have found that freebies will be valued at their cost.

We can always arrange a scholarship for the occasional person with real cash-flow problems, provided we impress the person with the fact that someone else is really subsidizing him. Besides, if the attendees don't pay, someone else must, and the chances of getting this subsidized by the diocese in these days of tight budgets are as close to zero as makes no difference. The total expense depends in part on how many people come, but the number coming will depend partly on what we charge. We come down to a best guess on what is reasonable, and a rather hairy act of faith in the outcome.

Another exercise in creative drudgery is getting presentors for the workshops. Most people in the field with the prestige and credibility to draw attendees are accustomed to a substantial reward for their time and are entitled to travel expenses. Finding people worth hearing, who are willing to come for what we can afford, is a challenge; this is another reason to start planning early.

Publicity

Getting the word out that we exist, or that we are putting on an event, is a real problem, partly because the people who need to hear it tend to hide in odd corners where they are hard to reach, and partly because those who should be spreading the word in person, such as clergy and mental health professionals, are usually so snowed-under with flyers from worthy causes that they simply discard them unread. This is even more of a challenge for us when the existing support groups only account for a bit over half the event attendance in our area. The solution lies in keeping clear on the difference between marketing and sales; advertising at the last moment is much less effective than keeping ourselves visible all year in the parish bulletins and diocesan and secular media. Don't forget the chancery office's courier service, which not only saves postage but lends a bit of official status. The divorce ministry in the diocese next door to mine made a lovely creative use of the courier service by conducting a survey about divorce issues among all the pastors: first a printed questionnaire on diocesan stationery, then a follow-up personal visit whether or not the pastor had returned the written form. Do they have everyone's attention? You betcha!

The smaller independent secular papers are another important resource; forget the big dailies—the ads are too expensive, and it's not effort-effective to wedge press releases in. The key is in personal contact, sufficient to ensure the editor recognizes us on the street, even when we're not trying to sell an article. Then we can much more easily get our human interest articles and letters to the editor printed, and the people we need to reach are more likely to notice us. The same applies to parish bulletins; while we need the pastor's approval, often the actual editor is the parish secretary, who accordingly comes in for a lot of appreciative attention especially when we don't happen to want a favor done.

The other standard publicity method is the brochure which, while not particularly cost-effective (figure maybe 2 or 3 percent will draw someone in and print quantities accordingly), does its part. Our region uses a legal-sized sheet printed both sides and folded in four panels, with a cover giving the nature of the event and its time and place, a listing of the workshops, the day's schedule, a map and directions, a tear-off registration form (make sure the form has nothing vital on its back side, such as the address . . . yes, we did, one year), and several phone numbers to call for more information. We begin saturating the area with these about three months before the conference date, via mailing lists, bulletin boards, parish bulletin inserts, laundromats, and wherever it is legal and visible to leave them about. It is NOT legal to put them in people's mailboxes. Be creative, but use common sense too.

Beginning Experience

Beginning Experience (BE) is a counterpart, for the healed divorcee, to the seven weeks for the newly divorced. BE is a separate organization from NACSDC, but the two work closely together and the facilitators are often also NACSDC members. The BE format is a very intense weekend, Friday night through Sunday afternoon, alternating group work with individual meditation and journalling, to close the door on the past and start a new, whole life. An individual can attend as many sessions as needed to achieve the purpose. BE can be an excellent preparation for one's annulment process (see below); we encourage people to hold off their annulments until they are ready for BE.

Services to Children of Divorced and Separated Parents

Divorce ministry is not complete, or even competent, until it addresses the needs of the children involved. Several recent studies have shown that the previous assumption that children get over it sooner and more easily is simply false, and that children of divorce in fact suffer worse and longer lasting devastation than their parents. This area within divorce ministry is fairly new, and much remains to be done even to get it properly started. Bear in mind that if half our marriages fail, we can expect a similar proportion of the children in our schools to be affected, which has obvious and fearful consequences both present and potential for the children and for our whole community.

Children's ministry is a good way to track down adult divorcees. One of the pastors contacted in the diocesan survey described above denied having any kind of "divorce problem" in his parish, but readily discussed how his school was full of children with single parents. The parish school is a great venue for recruiting, either as a subset of the parents' club or as an independent group.

Young Beginning Experience, conducted by BE, seeks to provide children with a place to express their hurts and concerns and support each other in a peer ministry of their own.

Another program is Rainbows for All God's Children, which is a young people's program similar to the seven weeks for adults. It is likewise becoming fashionable, particularly in Catholic high schools, to require a substantial commitment to community ministry both on campus and elsewhere, which can well be fulfilled by running a students' peer ministry support group on similar lines to the adult group.

Pastoral Resource

NACSDC can be, and in some places is, an excellent resource for pastoral staffs at parish and diocesan level to address many of the serious issues confronting today's Church. Persons completing the healing process tend to be both thoughtful and articulate about those issues and highly motivated to work on them. For example, an adequate premarital catechesis would put NACSDC out of business (nothing would please us more), and who could better design such a catechesis than someone for whom it has acquired a direct personal meaning? Likewise, we can debrief with the local tribunal and so help them understand the situation they confront. This is one area in which some active creativity could do some real good; we haven't begun to scratch the surface.

As another example of our services as a pastoral resource, NACSDC was invited to participate in the 1987 Bishops' Synod on The Vocation and Mission of the Laity in the Church and in the World. The resulting statement, *The Inner Journey of Catholics Who Separate, Divorce, or Remarry and the Outer Journey of Service to Others*, is well worth reading (see Appendix 3).

The Tribunal

In this country, many tribunals don't need telling about the pastoral aspect of their work; some, unfortunately, still need to think about it. In either case, the divorce minister will need to understand what the Tribunal does and why; the reading list at the end of this manual has some good books available on the subject, notably from Paulist Press, so we will give only a summary here.

The first point to make is that Church law, in practice, is not the adversarial, fault-finding affair that our civil law is.

For most of the canon lawyers I have met, pastoral considerations take precedence. We need to help our clients understand that approaching a Church court has very little in common with going to a civil court, apart from some of the jargon.

The reason for the tribunal's function is that the attempt to begin a marriage is a public event in the Christian community, which is called upon to witness it. When that attempt does not, in fact, result in a sacramental marriage (which is what a decree of nullity means), the Christian community has an interest in the outcome, both to remain clear on who is or is not married to whom (or is eligible to marry someone else) and to be alerted to the need for healing and reconciliation.

The tribunal's concern, with respect to the Christian community, is to affirm the sacrament of matrimony as what it is, and no other thing. With respect to the individual, the concern is to see what the problem was in order to resolve it and enable the person to go on with life healed and on the right track. There is absolutely no interest in any punitive or negatively judgemental content to the transaction. The only fault finding is with the bond itself, never with the parties to it.

The divorce minister will need to insist often and strongly that the Church does not "grant annulments" as the careless phrase has it. That is a synonym for allowing divorce. What the Church does is to "find nullity." The difference is that between ending something and finding that nothing was ever there; that the union was not one that God had joined together. This is not a minor nitpick, though some people have a problem grasping it. Likewise, nullity is not by any means found automatically, even in so-called liberal dioceses. The percentage of applications that result in decrees of nullity, which has recently attracted unhappy attention from Rome, is due in large part to the early discouragement of applicants who have no apparent case so as not to instill vain hopes and clog up the case load even worse than it already is.

Tribunal Procedure

The divorce minister will need to know something of the procedures used by the tribunal and of the grounds for nullity the tribunal will consider. We have seen applicants for an annulment somewhat taken aback by the phrasing of the decree when it arrived because they had not rightly understood what they were asking it to do. For example, having sought the civil divorce because the spouse was an alcoholic and had often been physically abusive, a friend of mine had some trouble with a decree of nullity based on their lack of emotional maturity at the time of the marriage. The distinction between the two kinds of action had not yet been clearly explained nor the connection between the two sets of grounds. This can cause some feelings of alienation from the Church, and the divorce minister will need to be very sensitive to the sometimes inconspicuous expressions of such feelings.

The procedure is simple. The applicant, whose civil divorce must already be final for obvious pastoral and legal reasons, can begin with the pastor in his or her own parish or a priest at another parish if preferred or may approach the tribunal directly. The first step by any route is a preliminary interview and questionnaire giving the essentials of the case and the proposed grounds for the annulment. The tribunal, on receiving this, will respond either with the paperwork for the next step or with an opinion that sufficient grounds do not seem to be present. If the latter, the applicant can start over if the matter seems to want clarification.

The paperwork for proceeding includes a request for witnesses who can testify about the parties at the time of the wedding, or later if this seems germane, and an outline for the applicant to follow in writing a statement on the case. The statement consists of a biography starting with childhood, a history of the relationship, and the applicant's feelings about what was defective in the marriage. The ex-spouse, if accessible, is informed of the procedure and asked to participate by doing the same paperwork; his or her cooperation is not necessary to proceed. Following receipt of the paperwork, the case then joins the queue to be considered, which can take several months depending on case load.

The tribunal's decision is reviewed automatically by another Church court for form, which normally occurs much more quickly, and the result is communicated to the spouses. The whole process is conducted by mail; applicants and witnesses do not attend the proceedings in person. There is usually a fee for the procedure; in most dioceses this covers only part of the actual costs and will be waived, without effect on the case, if the applicant is unable to pay.

Grounds for Finding Nullity

Grounds for nullity derive from the conditions necessary for any morally significant act: one must know what one is doing, one must be competent to do it, and one must choose freely to do it. Disparity of cult is an obvious impediment to knowledge, since a different belief system will involve a different notion of what marriage is. Being Catholic, by the way, is no guarantee against disparity in view of the ineffective catechesis noted elsewhere in this manual. Deception about the other's nature or intentions also invalidates a marriage. Impediments to competence include existing commitment to religious vows, holy orders, or marriage; being under age; or being mentally, emotionally, or physically incapable of married life. Impediments to free choice involve any kind of force or fear whether originating in another party or within the person attempting the marriage. Typical examples are marrying "because we have to" or to escape an abusive home. Any kind of mental reservation as to the nature or duties of Christian marriage is another, very common defect of choice, such as intending not to have children or not to raise them as Catholics, or intending some sort of "open marriage."

Please note that to say no sacrament took place is not in any way to say or imply that the couple were not sincere in their attempt or that they did not experience a deeply significant relationship. Some people feel the annulment process in some way belittles what has happened, and this is not at all its intent. The tribunal addresses only one aspect of the relationship, the sacramental bond, and does not (nor can it) pronounce on anything else about it.

Similarly, some people worry about the status of the children: does annulment make them illegitimate, for instance? Annulment has absolutely no effect on the children one way or another. "Legitimacy" is a purely civil concept arising from patrilinear inheritance of property and status and has nothing to do with a person's spiritual life. God has no illegitimate children; we're all adopted anyway!

The Family Life Office

Scope and Importance of Family Life Ministry

Working hand in hand with the tribunal and those responsible for catechesis, the Family Life Office can and should concern itself not only with the families that are still together, from primary school indoctrination of future spouses to grief counseling when one is widowed, but with failed marriages as well, from start to finish, and with the issues raised by both for the mode of the Church's presence in today's world. Unfortunately, some still don't. In such cases, persons seeking to do divorce ministry have a tough fight ahead. Before they can deal with the problem, they have to do a lot of consciousness-raising about its existence and nature (we hope this manual will contribute to that educational effort).

Marriage Preparation

Marriage preparation that confines itself to a few evenings of "discussion" with already-engaged couples is a waste of time, an insult to the Sacrament, and a major disservice to persons contemplating marriage. Intervention at that time is much too little, far too late. Education in Christian marriage must begin early; the catechesis for the Eucharist, for example, ought to discuss what a sacrament is that can lead to discussion later (such as when we teach the sixth commandment) of what we mean by calling marriage a sacrament. In teaching preadolescents about chastity and modest behavior, we must bear in mind that the whole point to that issue is marriage. It makes no sense to teach the "Thou shalt not . . . ." of it without also giving the positive side of what our sexuality is for. A series of unexplained negatives is not going to withstand the pressures of our culture to the contrary.

It is just here that we too often, and by long-standing tradition, fall flat on our faces. Please take note of how the world exerts its influence. It does not give a logical, abstract lecture on its point of view; it sells us stars and celebrities, convinces us that such persons are greatly to be admired and enthusiastically to be imitated, and then shows us how their wonderfulness consists precisely in their violating every standard of decency and right behavior.

Hollywood and Madison Avenue sell more drugs and lewdness, far more effectively, than the pushers and hookers on the street corner. If we abandon the field of ethical formation to these influences throughout our young people's adolescence and then try to tell a starry-eyed engaged couple about the right way to run a marriage, we simply make fools of ourselves. We need to compete vigorously with the world's subversions by marketing and selling a powerfully attractive alternative that will show up the world's celebrities for what they are before the young person's biological alarm clock goes off and, above all, to present role models that can stand against the peer pressure.

So far as the results of our efforts show, we have here a wide expanse of virtually blank paper. This is especially absurd when we consider that even our secular, materialist culture is itself visibly beginning to react against that same downward flow. Much that we see happening on the TV news every night can plausibly be read as a vast groping for something better, a great inarticulate craving for what is clean and life-giving. There has never been a better time for us to present the answer to that hunger and thirst for justice.

Until we see our tribunals in danger of shutting down for lack of business, we simply deceive ourselves if we think what we are already doing here, however strenuous and well motivated, is enough, especially when the same educational process that gives us high-probability candidates for divorce also produces the rest of the Catholic community, not excluding the clergy and the teachers who are to form the next generation in turn.

The Family Life Office functions right at the center of the most obvious part of the syndrome, which means it is ideally placed to shed some much needed light on the underlying disease itself. This is a huge responsibility, but it is also a magnificent opportunity—the greater the crisis, the more impact its successful resolution must have. The marriage crisis is the door to what could be a real golden age for the American Church, if we can get it open.

Divorce and Spirituality

The secular "New Age" movement has been dredging up a lot of useful material among the sludge. A good example is the very old notion of the "Wounded Healer," cf. Isaiah 53, under the title of "Shamanic Healing." A Shaman, properly speaking, is one who is called to undertake a journey into the center of his or her being, under a variety of adventurous and hazardous metaphors, and returns with greatly enhanced access to the powers that reside within all of us—that is, he or she can call out not only his or her own power but also the patient's. Healing consists of entering into the patient's predicament and leading the patient back out into wholeness. The parallel with the divorce minister should be sufficiently obvious as should the resemblance to Jungian theory and practice.

Note that our words "health," "wholeness," and "holiness" all come from the same linguistic root and that the concepts are still closely related. An approach to physical or emotional illness that concentrates on the disease as a thing in itself is a fine recipe for iatrogenic illness; the patient recovers in spite of the treatment, not because of it. The mind of Christ is to look at the whole person, and by extension the whole community, and treat that whole person as an integral being. This is clearly how Jesus works in the Gospels and how the early Church routinely acted. Jesus cured that whole person in line with St. Augustine's observation that "he became what we are that we might become what he is." He descended into our human condition in order to raise it up into nothing less than the inner life of the Blessed Trinity.

Divorce is a real descent into the Valley of the Shadow of Death, and its healing involves a real resurrection. A person so reborn can become a full fledged healer of the shamanic type, not only for other divorcees but for anyone who has been hurt, which is to say the entire unconverted human race. Such a person is a walking evangelion! We do not have the space to develop this theme adequately here; check out the reading list, starting with Morton Kelsey.

4

Conclusion

In an essay on the novels of H. G. Wells, Kenneth Rexroth says:

> Yet what happens? These heroic marriages always fail. [Wells's novels] are about . . . the failure of the last sacrament left to secular man, true marriage, in an all-corrupting social environment. This is not underlined in any propagandistic way. It is simply presented as the abiding tragedy of twentieth century man and woman . . . Who would be so optimistic today, as the century draws to its close, as to deny that, if love between a man and a woman is the last channel to the assumption of unlimited responsibility and realization, the Community of Love, it too has been choked up and is almost closed?
>
> —*More Classics Revisited* (New York: New Directions Publishing Corp., 1989) 130-31.

I chose this quotation from a decidedly non-Catholic writer, talking about a militant atheist who wrote ninety years ago, to underscore my point, not only that we face a genuine crisis but that it is an old crisis and a very obvious one. When St. Paul tells us the Christian family is a microcosm of the Church, one of the key ideas contained in that statement is the intimate nature of the bond and of the ministry. Marriage is not a "program"; it is one person meeting another. It is the same for the Church. Our religion is not a bureaucracy; it is the one Man, Jesus, meeting me one-on-one along the road to Emmaus or at Jacob's Well, and then my carrying the effect of that meeting out to my encounters with each of my neighbors so they can meet him too.

The troubles we listed for the Church, and for the person attempting marriage in contemporary America, all involve isolation and alienation of the members of the Mystical Body from each other. The cures must aim at getting them back together again—one by one. Our marriages don't take, too often, because we have lost the ability to touch each other and walk through life together. As individuals, we face isolation even from ourselves, and so the watchword of the mental health profession is personal integration. No program conceived in terms of body-count will cast out this demon; this is inescapably a matter for the sharing of grace between individuals. We need contagion, not congregation. Even the small group approach, of itself, guarantees nothing except possibly a stimulating evening's conversation once in a while. It is of value only so far as it encourages that channeling of grace.

The Ship of Peter never could afford to operate like a passenger liner; certainly in today's world there is no room for Christians who merely go through the motions without inner understanding or conviction. Even less is there occasion for a minority of uniformed professionals to do it all while the rest of us sit quietly and watch. The idea that the clergy were the real workers has always been an inversion of the gospel fostered by sheer momentum of numbers and custom. That momentum has dissipated, and we need to get back to the reality that we each are the workers in God's vineyard and that the clergy and religious minister to keep us functioning as such.

For both our secular neighbors and our uninvolved Christian siblings, there is an urgent need for some vigorous raising of consciousness. We need massive infusions of grace channeled one to one. We need to regain our sense of the numinous and so to restore the Christian mythos to its proper influence in our hearts. We need to regain our orientation, in educating ourselves and our young people, on that all-important encounter with Christ—not just to make a professional buzzword of it, as we too often do now, but to make it a visible reality among us. We need to quit wringing our institutional hands about the symptoms, such as the number of divorces and annulments, and start treating the disease by getting serious about who goes into marriage and why. We need to provide adequate support and encouragement to our engaged and married people, once they do begin their vocations properly.

Divorce ministry is ultimately about all of those things, not just about crying on each other's shoulders till we feel better. It makes us conscious of the fundamentals as few other things will, and it trains us superbly to address the true solutions in all their facets. The minister to divorced Catholics can take pride in being at the leading edge of the Church's life and in making a real difference to the bit of history going on just now. We pray the Spirit will send enough workers to take in the bountiful harvest we see before us.

Appendix 1

Preamble to the Constitution of the North American Conference of Separated and Divorced Catholics*

We, the members of the North American Conference of Separated and Divorced Catholics, dedicate ourselves to develop and expand a peer ministry within the Catholic community that offers encouragement, support, and education to all who experience a separation and divorce. While affirming always our traditional Catholic teaching and values on marriage and family life, we recognize with sadness that some Catholics may need to divorce and should then receive effective pastoral care from the Church. Further, we strive to create greater awareness among the separated and divorced that their anguish can become a source of new spiritual and personal growth for themselves and a source of grace for the whole community. We also endeavor to create greater awareness within the Church community that the pain and growth experienced by the separated and divorced person can enhance the Church's understanding of marriage as a sacrament and suffering as a Christian reality. As separated, divorced, and remarried Catholics, we invite the whole faith community to recognize and learn from our unique experience and to affirm that all separated, divorced, and remarried Catholics do truly belong within and have much to offer the Church community.

—Adopted by the NACSDC House of Delegates July 14, 1985

Note: The object of this statement was to state our goals clearly and succinctly. Several statements in it presume the reader's awareness of certain qualifiers; for instance, the word "remarried" does not mean we encourage someone to marry again without first obtaining a decree of nullity (see the discussion of the tribunal). It does mean that we seek to obtain a Christ-like attitude towards both the Catholic who remarries with an annulment of the previous attempt at marriage, but who still bears a totally unwarranted stigma in some quarters, and one who does so without the annulment. Such a case will not be improved by having the righteous look down their noses, especially where there has been false information about the legitimate options within the Church. BOTH are entitled to outreach and healing.

Appendix 2

Resources and Contacts

North American Conference of Separated
  and Divorced Catholics
Central Office
1100 S. Goodman St.
Rochester, NY 14620
(716) 271-1320

Beginning Experience
Central Office
305 Michigan Ave.
Detroit, MI 48226
(313) 965-5110

Rainbows for All God's Children
1111 Tower Rd.
Schaumburg, IL 60173-4305

Retrouvaille
15230 Las Robles
Oak Forest, IL 60452

Nolo Press
950 Parker St.
Berkeley, CA 94710

Appendix 3

FOR FURTHER STUDY

The following books are available in paperback, either at bookstores, libraries, or from the publishers. The list is far from exhaustive. If you do not live near a good bookstore, the NACSDC catalog will keep you busy reading for a year or so. NACSDC can also put you in touch with a member who can shop for you.

Eugene Skelton, *The Ministry to the Small-Group Leader* (Collegeville: The Liturgical Press, 1987).

Merrill Morse, *The Ministry to the Single Person* (Collegeville: The Liturgical Press, 1988).

Both should be read together, along with this manual.

Also helpful are:

I. Gramunt, J. Hervada, and L. Wauk, *Canons and Commentaries on Marriage* (Collegeville: The Liturgical Press, 1987) and Geoffrey Robinson, *Marriage, Divorce & Nullity: A Guide to the Annulment Process in the Catholic Church* (Collegeville: The Liturgical Press, 1984).

The Plan of Pastoral Action for Family Ministry: A Vision and Strategy (Washington: United States Catholic Conference [3211 4th Street N.E., 20017-1194] 1978).

A single-sheet introductory brochure and the statement to the Bishops' Synod mentioned on p. 49 are available from the central office of the North American Conference of Separated and Divorced Catholics, 1100 S. Goodman St., Rochester, NY 14620. While you're at it, ask for a current catalog of books and tapes.

James Young, *Divorcing, Believing, Belonging* (Mahwah, N.J.: Paulist Press, [987 Macarthur Blvd., 07430] 19--). Good introductory book on divorce issues by the man who invented divorce ministry.

The Canon Law Society of America, *The Code of Canon Law: A Text and Commentary* (Mahwah, N.J.: Paulist Press, 1983). You will be interested in Canons 1055–1165 on marriage, its nature, and the impediments to it, and 1671–1707 on the marriage tribunal.

Faculty of Canon Law, *Handbook II for Marriage Nullity Cases* (Ottawa: St. Paul University, 1980). Superb treatment on what marriage is all about by way of background to handling cases that weren't marriages. A must-have for the serious divorce minister.

Charles Sherman, *How to Do Your Own California Divorce* (Berkeley: Nolo Press [950 Parker St., Berkeley, CA 94710] updated annually). The first point this book makes, and that very strongly, is that while law *in pro per* is a great idea and every citizen's right, it isn't always the smart way to go in the real world. Still, if you live in California, get and read this before you see the lawyer. If you live elsewhere, write to Nolo for suggestions about where you live (resources, books, etc).

Herb Cohen, *You Can Negotiate Anything* (New York: Bantam [666 5th Ave., 10103] 1980). The standard text for win/win negotiating. Don't be deceived by the chatty tone and small size; the man knows what he's talking about.

Edward Whitmont, *The Symbolic Quest* (Princeton, N.J.: Princeton University Press, 1978). Widely regarded as the best lay people's introduction to Jungian personality theory, which makes a useful underpinning to wounded-healer spirituality.

Charles L Whitfield, *Healing the Child Within* (Deerfield Beach, Fl.: Health Communications, Inc., 1987). Good treatment of adult children of dysfunctional families and of one approach to recovery.

Robert A Johnson, *He, She, We, Ecstasy* and *Inner Work* (New York: Harper & Row [10 E. 53rd St., 10022], 19--). Despite the cutesy titles, these books contain useful insight on issues pertinent to divorce ministry. *We* is a good treatment of the romantic heresy.

Denis de Rougemont, *Love in the Western World* (New York: Harper & Row [10 E. 53rd St., 10022] 1974). The standard full-length treatment of romantic love. A must-read, despite his being a bit of a crank.

Elizabeth Kübler-Ross, *On Death and Dying* (New York: Collier Macmillan [866 3rd Ave., 10022] 1970). The classic text. As noted in her book, the same principles apply to any major loss; one would grieve being fired from one's job in the same way.